ChordTime® Piano

Favorites

Level 2B

I-IV-V⁷ chords in keys of C, G and F

I-IV-V^7 chords in keys of C, G and F

This book belongs to: _____

Arranged by

Nancy and Randall Faber

Production: Frank and Gail Hackinson
Production Coordinator: Marilyn Cole
Design: Terpstra Design, San Francisco
Music Editor: Edwin McLean
Engraving: Music Craft of Hollywood, Inc. (Fla.)

FABER
PIANO ADVENTURES®
3042 Creek Drive
Ann Arbor, Michigan 48108

A NOTE TO TEACHERS

ChordTime® Piano Favorites is a collection of favorite folk songs and familiar melodies arranged for the Level 2B pianist. This delightful supplementary book offers pieces useful for recital performances, family or group sing-along, and as motivational material for the private or group lesson.

As the title *ChordTime®* suggests, the emphasis of this book is on the student's mastery of I, IV, and V⁷ chords. The pieces are arranged in the keys of C, G, and F with warm-up exercises for each key. Different accompanying styles have been chosen to expand the student's recognition and application of these chords.

ChordTime® Piano Favorites is part of the *ChordTime® Piano* series arranged by Faber and Faber. "ChordTime" designates Level 2B of the *PreTime® to BigTime® Supplementary Library,* and it is available in a variety of styles.

Following are the levels of the supplementary library which lead from *PreTime®* to *BigTime®.*

PreTime® Piano	(Primer Level)
PlayTime® Piano	(Level 1)
ShowTime® Piano	(Level 2A)
ChordTime® Piano	(Level 2B)
FunTime® Piano	(Level 3A – 3B)
BigTime® Piano	(Level 4)

Each level offers books in a variety of styles, making it possible for the teacher to offer stimulating material for every student. For a complimentary detailed listing, e-mail faber@pianoadventures.com or write us at the mailing address below.

Visit **www.PianoAdventures.com**.

Helpful Hints:

1. The chord warm-ups for a given key should be played daily before practicing the songs.

2. The student can be asked to identify the I, IV, and V⁷ chords in each song and write the correct chord symbol below the bass staff.

3. Hands-alone practice is recommended to facilitate correct fingering and accurate rhythm.

ISBN 978-1-616-77-014-3

TABLE OF CONTENTS

I, IV, V⁷ Chords in Key of C

Skip to My Lou 4

Three Blind Mice 6

The Mexican Clapping Song 8

Rise and Shine 10

The Great Meat Pie 12

I, IV, V⁷ Chords in Key of G

The Duke of York 14

Everybody Loves Saturday Night 16

Long, Long Ago 18

Down by the Riverside 20

I, IV, V⁷ Chords in Key of F

Auld Lang Syne 22

Where Has My Little Dog Gone? 24

Hot Cross Buns 25

Turkey in the Straw........................... 26

America 28

Dictionary of Musical Terms 29

FF1014

Key of C

Practice these warm-ups before playing the songs in the key of C.

Warm-up 1

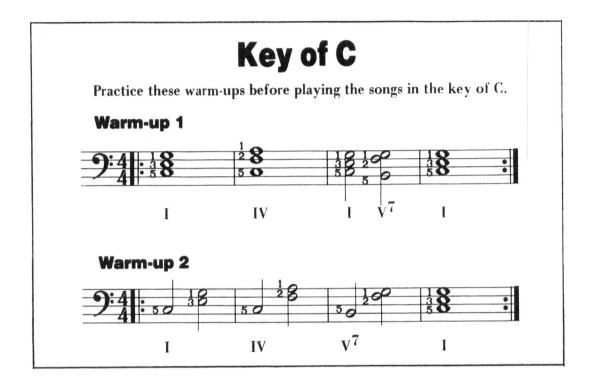

Warm-up 2

Skip to My Lou

Southern Mountain Song

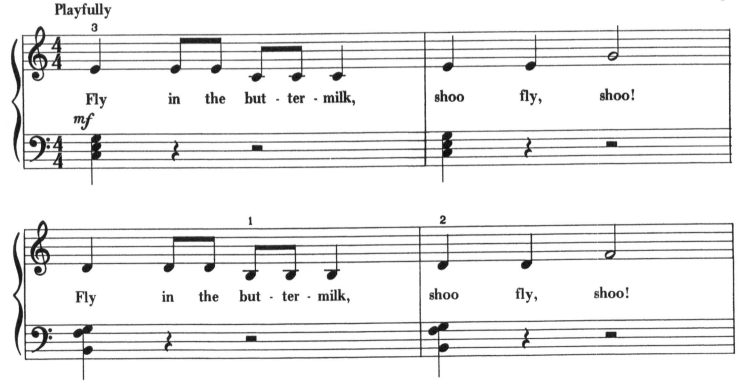

Playfully

Fly in the but-ter-milk, shoo fly, shoo!

mf

Fly in the but-ter-milk, shoo fly, shoo!

Three Blind Mice

Traditional

Scampering along

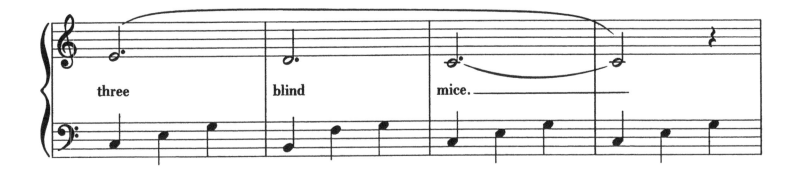

all ran down to the store one night and

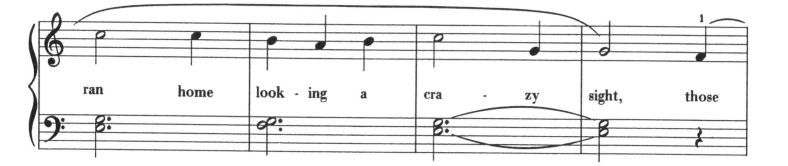

bought eye - glass - es to help their sight. They

ran home look - ing a cra - zy sight, those

three blind mice.

mf

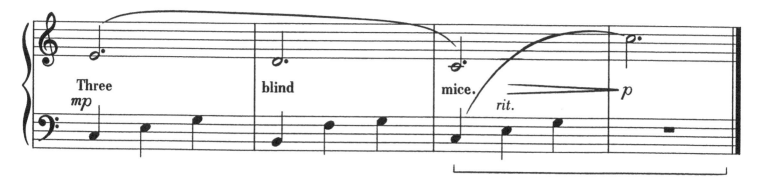

Three blind mice.

mp *rit.* *p*

The Mexican Clapping Song

Mexican Folk Song

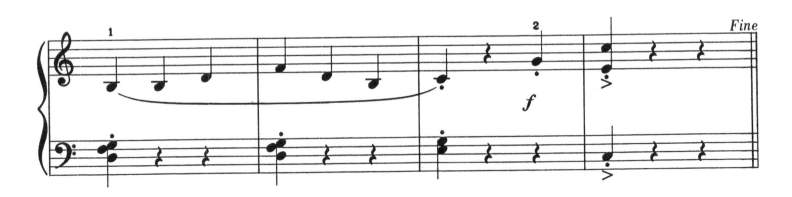

2122222222222

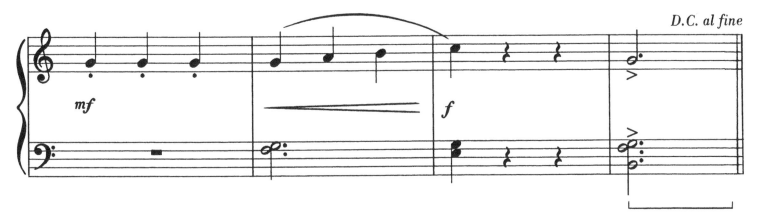

FF1014

Rise and Shine

American Folk Song

FF1014

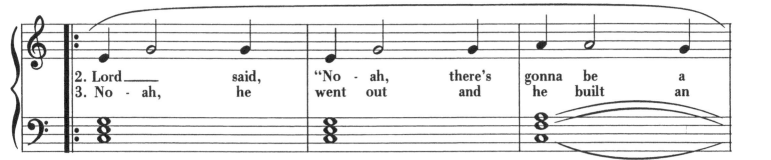

2. Lord____ said, "No - ah, there's gonna be a
3. No - ah, he went out and he built an

flood - y, flood - y, Lord____ said "No - ah, there's
ark - y, ark - y, No - ah, he went out and

gonna be a flood - y, flood - y, Get your chil - dren
he built an ark - y, ark - y. Made it out of

out of the mud - dy, mud - dy, Chil - dren of the
hick - o - ry bark - y, bark - y,

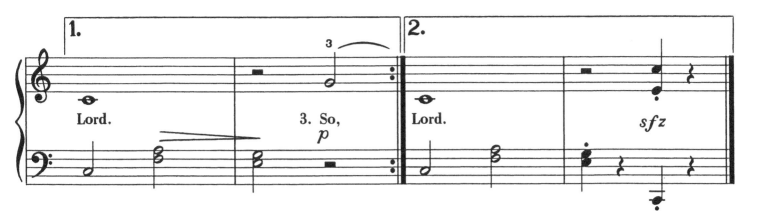

1.
Lord. 3. So,

2.
Lord. sfz

The Great Meat Pie

British Folk Song
(Adapted)

Proudly

great meat pie was a mon - ster size, and it
took full thir - ty _____ sacks of flour, it's a

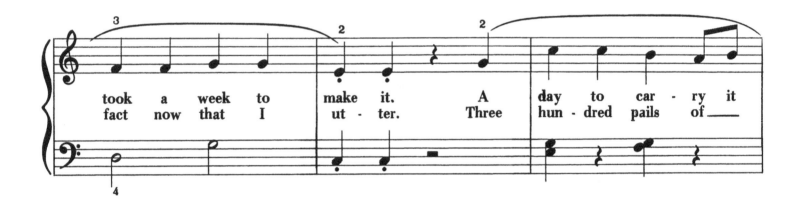

took a week to make it. A day to car - ry it
fact now that I ut - ter. Three hun - dred pails of _____

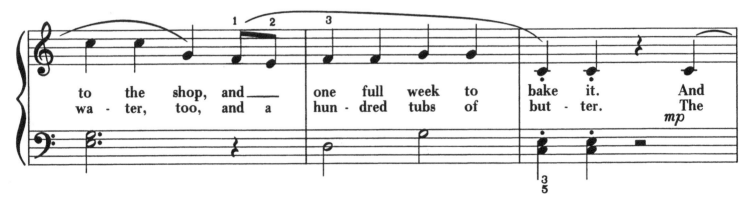

to the shop, and _____ one full week to bake it. And
wa - ter, too, and a hun - dred tubs of but - ter. The

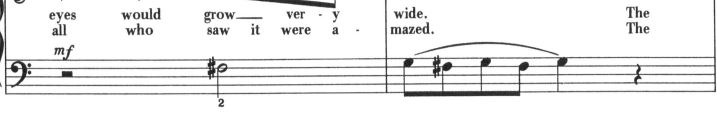

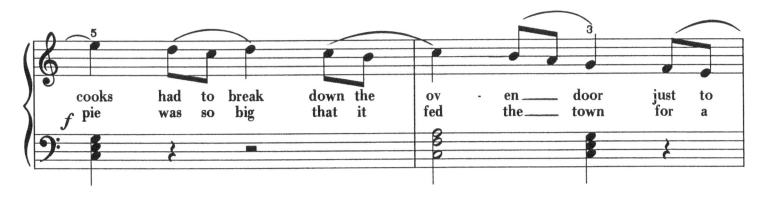

Key of G

Practice these warm-ups before playing the songs in the key of G.

The Duke of York

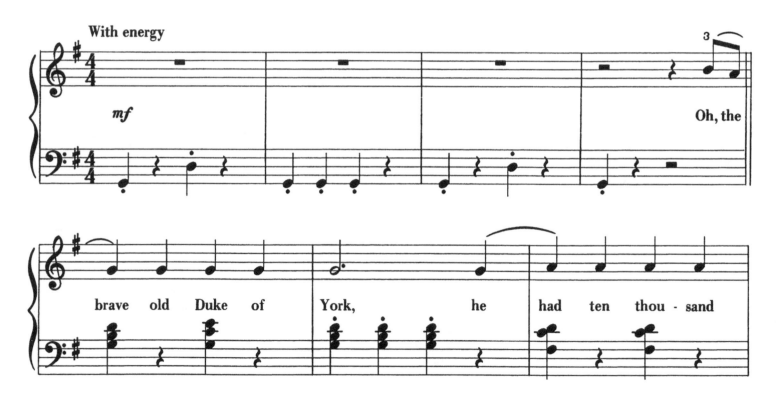

men; He marched them to the top of the hill and he

marched them down a - gain. And ___ when they were up they were

up, and when they were down they were down. And

when they were just half - way up, they were nei - ther up nor down.

mf *p*

8va

FF1014

Everybody Loves Saturday Night

West African Folk Song

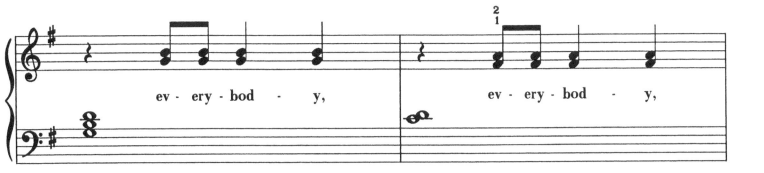

ev - ery - bod - y,   ev - ery - bod - y,

Ev - ery - bod - y   loves   Sat - ur - day

night.

Ev - ery - bod - y   loves   Sat - ur - day   night.

Long, Long Ago

Thomas H. Bayly

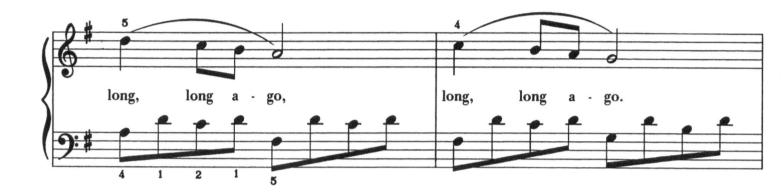

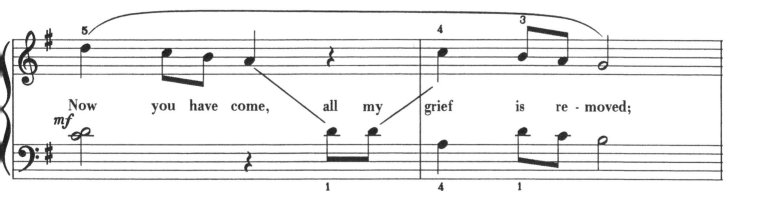

Now you have come, all my grief is re - moved;

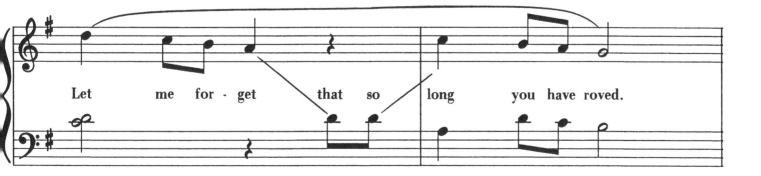

Let me for - get that so long you have roved.

Let me be - lieve that you love as you loved,

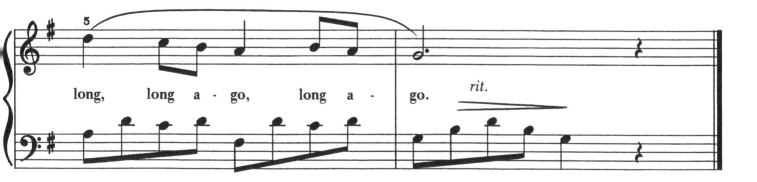

long, long a - go, long a - go. *rit.*

Down by the Riverside

Spiritual

With spirited swing

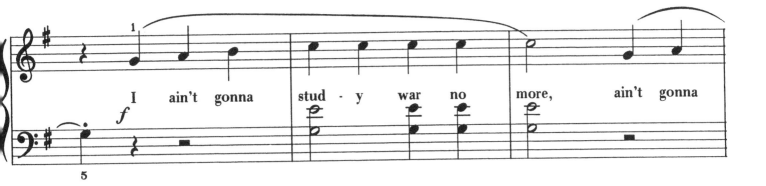

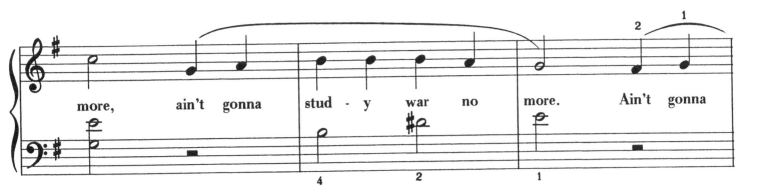

Key of F

Practice these warm-ups before playing the songs in the key of F.

Warm-up 1

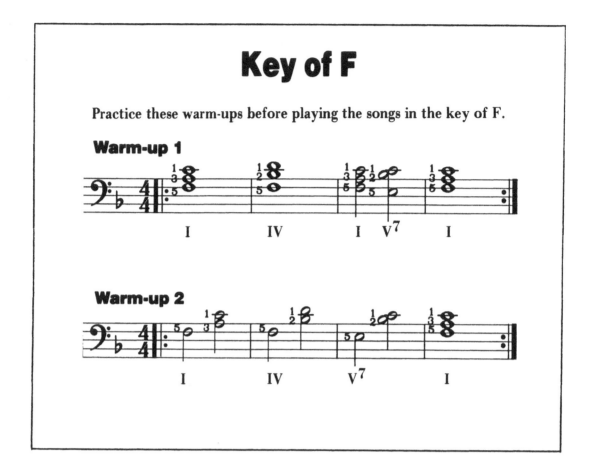

Warm-up 2

Auld Lang Syne

Slowly

Traditional

Should auld ac‐quaint‐ance be for‐got, and

nev‐er brought to mind, Should auld ac‐quaint‐ance

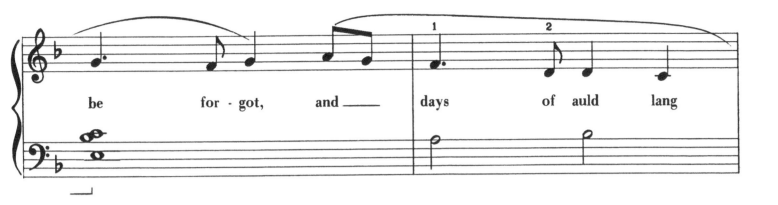

be for - got, and _____ days of auld lang

syne? For auld _____ lang _____ syne, my dear, for

auld _____ lang _____ syne, We'll take a cup of

kind - ness yet for _____ auld _____ lang _____ syne.

Where Has My Little Dog Gone?

Traditional

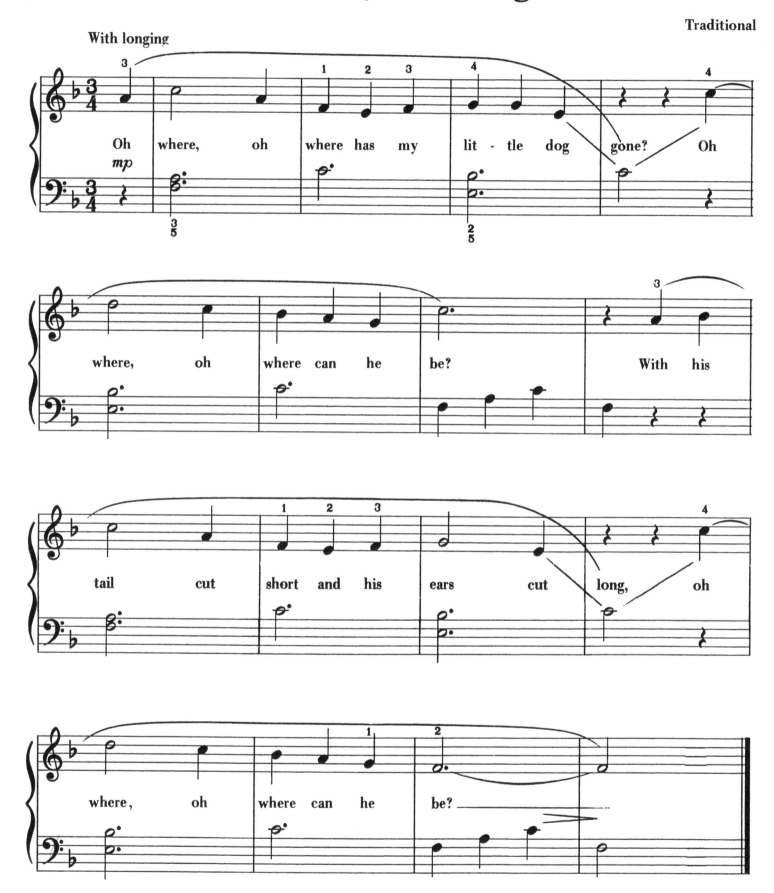

Hot Cross Buns

British Folk Song

FF1014

Turkey in the Straw

American Folk Song

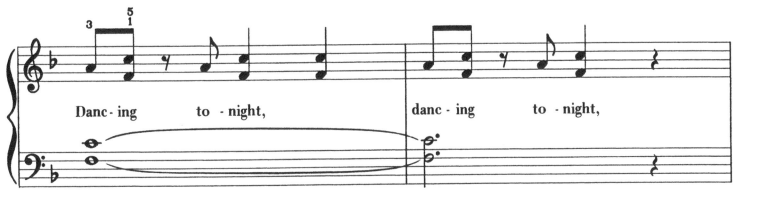

Danc - ing to - night, danc - ing to - night,

Danc - ing to - night, danc - ing to - night.

Pret - tiest gal you ev - er saw will be danc - ing with me to the
(guy)

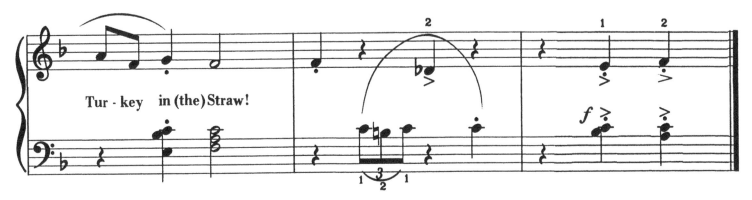

Tur - key in (the) Straw!

America

Rev. Samuel F. Smith

Proudly

My coun - try 'tis of thee, sweet land of lib - er - ty,

mf

of thee I sing. Land where my fa - thers died,

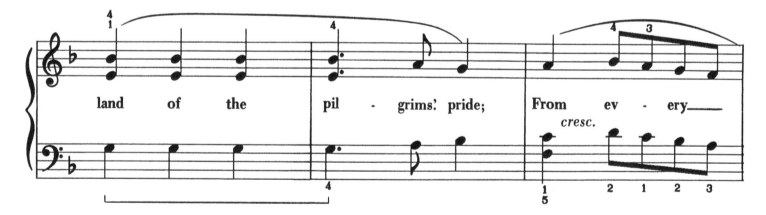

land of the pil - grims' pride; From ev - er - y

cresc.

moun - tain - side, let free - dom ring.

f